Titles in this series
Big J
Clever Cleo
Don't Say No To Flo
Gunpowder Guy
Hal the Hero
The Little Queen
Will's Dream
William's Words

Text copyright © Stewart Ross 2002
Illustrations copyright © Sue Shields 2002

Series concept: Stewart Ross
Series editor: Alex Woolf
Editor: Liz Gogerly
Book Design: Design Systems

The picture of William Shakespeare on page 30 belongs to the Hodder Wayland Picture Library.

Published in Great Britain by Hodder Wayland, an imprint of Hodder Children's Books

British Library Cataloguing in Publication Data
Ross, Stewart
William's Words : the story of William Shakespeare. - (Stories from history)
1. Shakespeare, William, 1564-1616
2. Theatre - England - History - 16th century - Juvenile literature
I. Title II. Shields, Susan
822.3'3

ISBN 0 7502 3274 9

Printed and bound in Hong Kong by Sheck Wah Tong Printing Press Ltd

Hodder Children's Books
A division of Hodder Headline Limited
338 Euston Road, London NW1 3BH

William's Words

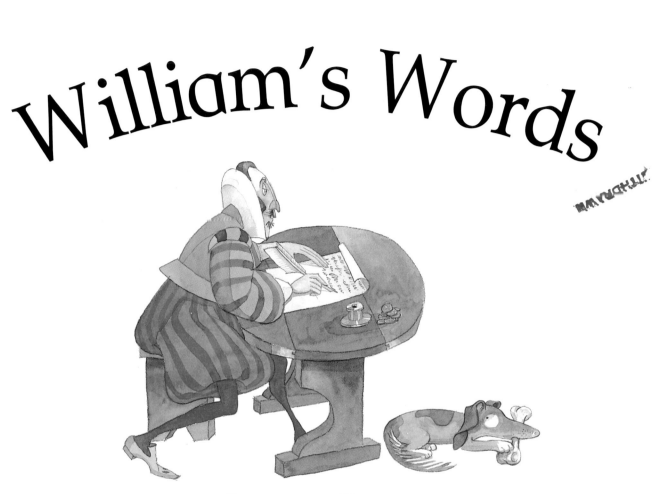

Stewart Ross
Illustrated by Sue Shields

HODDER
Wayland

an imprint of Hodder Children's Books

William loved words.

He liked plays, too.

William also liked girls.

Anne and William were married.

They had three children …

but not much money.

William did not like his job.

He went to London.

William worked in the theatre.

He helped the actors.

He learned all about the theatre ...

and he saw many plays.

William was a good actor, too.

But he did not like the plays.

William wrote his own play.

The actors liked William's play.

The crowds liked it, too.

William wrote lots more plays.

Some were funny ...

and some were sad.

The queen heard about William's plays.

She wanted to see one of William's plays.

The queen said William's play …

was the best she had ever seen.

When William came home …

he was a rich man.

Do you know?

This story is TRUE!
William was WILLIAM SHAKESPEARE.
He wrote about 38 plays. Today they are put on all over the world.
He lived almost 400 years ago. He died in 1616.
We think this is what he looked like:

Notes for adults

William's Words and the National Curriculum

William's Words may be enjoyed in its own right or, in school, as part of a programme of reading and study linked to the National Curriculum. To this end, the language, content and presentation have been devised to meet the requirements of the *National Literacy Strategy* and *Key Stage 1 English and History*. Whether read by an individual pupil or by the teacher out loud, *William's Words* makes a stimulating addition to material available for the Literacy Hour. It skilfully combines development of the 'knowledge, skills and understanding' and 'breadth of study' required by the *English National Curriculum* (pp. 18-19) with 'chronological understanding', 'knowledge and understanding of events, people and changes in the past' and learning about 'the lives of significant men, women and children drawn from the history of Britain and the wider world' and 'past events from the history of Britain and the wider world' suggested in the *History National Curriculum*.

Suggested follow-up activities

1. Checking the child knows and can use words they might not have come across before. In particular:

Wonderful	actor	Majesty	goodbye	exit
twins	mistakes	paid	careful	angel
quiet	cakes	married	ado	Juliet
London	Romeo	wise	funny	
farewell	voice	horse	crowds	
theatre	dagger	sorry	laugh	

2. Talking about tangible objects that survive from Elizabethan England, e.g. buildings (Anne Hathaway's Cottage, etc.), manuscripts and everyday objects such as jewellery. The reconstructed Globe is, of course, a vital modern monument. Discussing how we know about Elizabethan England, i.e. sources (perhaps looking at an early printed play).

3. Explaining the exact dates of Shakespeare's life and discussing other characters in the story, i.e. Anne Hathaway, Elizabeth I, Christopher Marlowe.

4. Going further into aspects of Elizabethan England. e.g. development of drama and theatres, Queen Elizabeth, buildings, education, literacy, dress, etc.

5. Comparing life in Elizabethan England with our own times, e.g. costume, health and disease, travel, housing, religion, theatre, etc.